I Can Draw KAWAII People

sourcebooks
wonderland

T0011071

Copyright © Green Android Ltd, 2022
Illustrations by Ksenya Savva
Additional illustrations courtesy of www.dreamstime.com

First edition for the United States and Canada published by:
Sourcebooks Wonderland, an imprint of Sourcebooks Kids
P.O. Box 4410, Naperville, Illinois 60567-4410
(630) 961-3900
sourcebookskids.com

Sourcebooks and the colophon are registered trademarks of Sourcebooks

All rights reserved.

The art was first sketched, then painted digitally with brushes designed by the artist.

Library of Congress Cataloging-in-Publication Data is on file with the publisher.

Source of Production: WKT Company Limited, Hong Kong
Date of Production: August 2022
Run Number: 001

Printed and bound in China.
HH 10 9 8 7 6 5 4 3 2 1

I Can Draw KAWAII People

Illustrated by **Ksenya Savva**

In a Kawaii world, everything is cute, kind, and happy.

What's inside this Kawaii wonderland?

18 Caring vet

20 Fearless firefighter

22 Diligent detective

24 Creative chef

26 Cute baby

38 Ace racer

40 Speedy snowboarder

42 Intrepid explorer

44 Working cowboy

46 Marvelous medic

58 Amazing mechanic

60 Portrait artist

62 Fantastic farmer

Which Kawaii character are you going to draw now?

What you need

The tools needed for *I CAN DRAW KAWAII* are few and you are bound to have them all.

drawing pencil

eraser

pencil sharpener

white paper so you can draw all your favorite Kawaii people again and again

coloring pencils or marker pens

How to draw cool Kawaii people

Work through the five easy steps, starting with number 1.
Each step is made up of lines or simple shapes. Take your time and
don't press heavily on the pencil—pale lines are easier to erase.

1.

Make your drawing on
the practice page the
same size as here.

2.

Only draw what is
shown in black lines.

3.

Gray dots
indicate lines
to be rubbed
out with
the eraser.

4.

Gray lines show
what you have
drawn in
previous steps.

5.

Look closely
when drawing
small details.

Here is a finished Kawaii
character. Follow this when
coloring your drawing.

When you have finished
your drawing and you are
happy with it, you can
go over the outlines in
black before coloring.

Don't forget to
read the idea
bubble on the
practice page.

Super superhero

A superhero's work is never done because there is always someone, somewhere in the world who needs help. Are you a superhero?

1.

2.

draw a U-shape

3.

make the hair curly

erase dotted lines

4.

don't forget the cape

5.

WOW

wham

pow

draw your superhero

boom

Look, it's your superhero flying over a city. Draw the skyscrapers, towers, and apartments.

Cool skateboarder

There are a lot of skateboard tricks, but this boarder
knows you must nail drop-ins, kick turns, and tic-tacs first.

1.

2.

erase

3.

draw the
skateboard

4.

add the
cool hood

add both
arms

erase

5.

draw your
skateboarder

yeah

Skateboard decks
are covered with
cool pictures and
lettering. Design and
draw a lot on this page.

Clever scientist

In their laboratories, scientists carry out experiments that can save lives. Imagine if you created a medicine that made people better.

1.

2. add bangs

3. erase

4. protective goggles are a must

5. erase dots

add a flask

12

I can draw Kawaii people

draw your scientist

Your scientist is very busy in the lab. Surround her with more tubes and flasks.

Junior gamer

Junior gamer is creating an imaginary world with materials and tools she discovers on her journey.

1.

2.

draw two ovals and a circle

3.

erase

add the controller

now draw wavy hair

4.

erase

add microphone tip

5.

14

I can draw Kawaii people

draw your
gamer

Nasty invaders want
to ruin the gamer's
imaginary world.
Draw a lot of
pixel creatures.

15

Star astronaut

Imagine being an astronaut and spacewalking among twinkling stars and zooming asteroids with our planet earth hundreds of miles below.

1.

2.

draw ovals

3.

erase dotted lines

4.

add arms and legs

5.

add spacesuit details

draw your astronaut

Practice page

Try drawing a space rocket with a cable attached to your spacewalking astronaut.

17

Caring vet ✚

Caring for sick and injured animals is hard. As animal patients can't speak, the vet must work out what is wrong.

1.

2.
erase
draw headlamp band

3.
add the lamp

4.

5.
a purrfect patient

draw your vet

It's a busy day at the surgery. Draw animals that need your vet's expert care.

Fearless firefighter

Within minutes of an alarm, firefighters must be suited up
and ready in the fire truck. Every second counts in an emergency.

1.

2.

draw the brim
of the helmet

3.

look out for
the dotted
lines to erase

4.

add the
hose

5.

20

draw your firefighter

Draw a bright red fire truck with its flashing light on the roof and a ladder, ready to use.

Diligent detective

The detective is on a mission. Her task is to hunt down and find the cat burglar. To succeed will take all her skill.

1.

2. erase

draw an oval for the hat brim

3. add the crown of the hat

4. add the magnifying glass

5. add jacket details

23

Creative chef

This chef is a whiz at making everything from yummy cakes to warming casseroles. What do you like to create in the kitchen?

1.

2. draw the top of the chef's hat

3. erase

4. add the hair — erase

5. draw the ladle

24

draw your chef

Chef is ready to prep the ingredients. Draw a lot of cute Kawaii vegetable characters.

Cute baby

Babies are adorable—even when they cry—and need all the love and tender care possible. What would you name this baby?

1.

2.

draw two ears

3.

add a cute bow

4.

curly wisp of hair

5.

tiny baby tears

26

draw your baby

Turn those tears into a smile by surrounding baby with her favorite toys and cuddly friend.

Helpful hero

Police officers promise to serve and protect the community by catching wrongdoers and much more. They wear their uniform with pride.

1.

2. draw an oval for the hat top

3. erase

4. add a belt buckle and tie

5. add a lot of curly hair

draw your
police officer

This police officer
is ready to leave
the station and go
on patrol. Draw
the police car.

Nimble ninja

This ninja is practicing judo and karate kata moves against an imaginary opponent. A ninja has to be very fit!

add the ninja headtie

1.

2.

3.

4.

5.

erase dotted lines

add toy nunchaku

draw your ninja

A ninja must have great balance. Draw your ninja practicing his moves on a rooftop.

Pesky pirate

Arrr, it's high jinks on the high seas! There is always mischief afoot when this pirate is at the helm.

1.

2. erase

draw the tricorn hat's outer brim

3. add inner brim

4.

5. remember the hook

draw your
pirate

Look at the pirate's
treasure! Draw a
treasure chest filled
with gold coins.

Singing sensation

Imagine being a pop star with fans cheering and clapping, waiting to hear your latest hit.

1.

draw a circle

2.

erase dotted line

3.

4.

every pop star needs a microphone

5.

add the microphone stand

34

I can draw Kawaii people

draw your
pop star

In concert tonight

....

Give your pop star
a name, and then
design and decorate
a huge poster
showing his name.

35

Marathon runner

A marathon is a 26.2-mile race. The record time for a marathon is two hours, one minute and 39 seconds. Wow!

1.

2.
draw the sweatband

3.
add hair

erase all dotted lines

4.
add sweatbands to wrist

5.

draw your runner

finishing time

hours	mins	secs
:	:	

He won! Draw the runner crossing the marathon line. Write his marathon time in the digital watch.

37

Ace racer

This ace racer is ready to rev, working his way through the gears as he roars around the track. Good luck!

1.

2. erase

draw the hair

3.

4.

5.

finish ace racer's overalls

draw a helmet

draw your racing driver

An ace racer needs an ace car. Design and draw one that will win races.

Speedy snowboarder

This awesome snowboarder wears cool gear, and makes turns, ramps, half pipes, and jumps look easy.

1.

draw a circle

2.

3.

draw the goggles

4.

add legs

5.

add the snowboard

erase

draw your
snowboarder

Draw your
snowboarder in
mid-air coming off
a snow-covered hill.
Put mountains in
the background.

Intrepid explorer

This explorer is trekking across the hot savannah studying the plants and animals. Would you like to be an explorer?

1.

2. draw an oval

3. draw a curved line
erase dotted lines

4. add a pair of binoculars

5. draw an explorer's map
erase

draw your
explorer

Draw the explorer's
campsite with tent,
table and chair, and
a fire for cooking.

Working cowboy

A working cowboy herds livestock, repairs fences, and cares for his horse. A cowboy has to be a great rider.

1.

2.

draw the rim of the Stetson

draw waistcoat front

3.

4.

erase

every cowboy needs a neckerchief

5.

erase

draw your cowboy

Draw your cowboy's horse, saddled up and ready for a day driving cattle.

Marvelous medic

It takes years of study to become a doctor.
There is so much to learn about the human body.

1.

draw a
circle

2.

3.

draw arms
and legs

4.

erase

add
detail to
the coat

add the
medic's
chart

5.

the all-important
stethoscope

draw your medic

The doctor is doing her rounds. Draw the ward that she works in.

Super slugger

The bases are loaded. The pitcher is ready.
It's time for star slugger to hit one out of the park.

1.

2. draw the batting helmet brim

3. add the baseball bat   erase

4. draw hair

5.

draw your hitter

Draw the pitcher winding up ready to throw a curveball to your star slugger.

Perfect princess

This fairy-tale princess is dressed in her finest clothing.
Which royal occasion do you think she is attending?

1.

2. draw hair
in a bun

3.

draw arms
and long
skirt

4. add a
tiara

add a frill

5.

add more
frills

draw your
princess

Draw the princess's
fairy-tale castle
complete with towers,
arched windows,
huge doors, and
a lot of flags.

Construction worker

On a construction site there are engineers, crane drivers, scaffolders, carpenters, and more. All must wear a protective hard hat.

1.

2.

3. draw ridge in the hat

erase

draw the hard hat's peak

4. draw a plank of wood

5. add a hammer

a handy pocket

52

draw your construction worker

Draw the carpenter at work. You choose what he is making and give him the tools he will need.

Magnificent magician

Abracadabra! Alakazam! What tricks will the magician perform?
Will he make a coin disappear or pull something from his top hat?

1.

2.
erase

3.
draw the hat top and brim

draw arms and cape

4.
erase

5.
draw a magic wand

add a bow tie

54

draw your
magician

The magician has
waved his wand.
Draw a rabbit
sitting on the
magician's top hat.

Airline pilot

The pilot pushes the throttle forward, the engines roar, and the plane takes off. Choose a destination for this flight.

1.

2.

3. erase

4. start to draw the cap badge

add a collar and tie

5. captain's epaulettes

add details to the shirt

draw your pilot

It's a busy day at the airport. Draw aircraft, large and small, taking off and coming in to land.

57

Amazing mechanic

When a car breaks down, you need a mechanic to look under the hood. A good mechanic can fix any engine!

1.

2.

3.

erase

draw cap brim

4.

add detail to the overalls

5.

a handy spanner

add a toolbox

58

draw your mechanic

Draw an engine that needs a refit and the tools the mechanic will need.

Portrait artist

A portrait artist aims to depict the sitter's appearance and character. Would you like to have your portrait painted?

1.

2. draw an oval

3. erase

4.
add a paintbrush
draw an outline of the hair
add a palette

5.
make the hair wavy
erase

draw your artist

Draw yourself sitting for your portrait. Don't forget to draw the artist's canvas and easel, and paint palette.

Fantastic farmer

A farmer's day is a long one. There is so much to do—animals to feed and crops to plant and harvest.

1.

2. draw a curved line

3. draw hat top and brim
erase

4. finish the brim

5. draw plaited hair
add an essential pitchfork
erase

Name the farm. Write it here.

Farm

62